A R o b b i e R e a d e r

ADRIAN PETERSON

Karen Bush Gibson

KING COUNTY LIBRARY SYSTEM, WA

Mitchell Lane
PUBLISHERS

P.O. Box 196
Hockessin, Delaware 19707
Visit us on the web: www.mitchelllane.com
Comments? email us: mitchelllane@mitchelllane.com

Mitchell Lane
PUBLISHERS

Printing   1   2   3   4   5   6   7   8   9

A Robbie Reader Biography

Abigail Breslin	Dr. Seuss	Mia Hamm
Adrian Peterson	Dwayne "The Rock" Johnson	Miley Cyrus
Albert Einstein	Dwyane Wade	Miranda Cosgrove
Albert Pujols	Dylan & Cole Sprouse	Philo Farnsworth
Alex Rodriguez	Eli Manning	Raven-Symoné
Aly and AJ	Emily Osment	Roy Halladay
AnnaSophia Robb	Emma Watson	Selena Gomez
Amanda Bynes	Hilary Duff	Shaquille O'Neal
Ashley Tisdale	Jaden Smith	Story of Harley-Davidson
Brenda Song	Jamie Lynn Spears	Sue Bird
Brittany Murphy	Jennette McCurdy	Syd Hoff
Charles Schulz	Jesse McCartney	Taylor Lautner
Chris Johnson	Jimmie Johnson	Tiki Barber
Cliff Lee	Johnny Gruelle	Tim Lincecum
Dakota Fanning	Jonas Brothers	Tom Brady
Dale Earnhardt Jr.	Jordin Sparks	Tony Hawk
David Archuleta	Justin Beiber	Troy Polamalu
Demi Lovato	Keke Palmer	Victoria Justice
Donovan McNabb	Larry Fitzgerald	
Drake Bell & Josh Peck	LeBron James	

Library of Congress Cataloging-in-Publication Data
Gibson, Karen Bush.
 Adrian Peterson / by Karen Bush Gibson.
    p. cm. — (A robbie reader)
 Includes bibliographical references and index.
 ISBN 978-1-61228-060-8 (library bound)
 1. Peterson, Adrian—Juvenile literature. 2. Football players—United States—Biography—Juvenile literature. I. Title.
 GV939.P477G53 2012
 796.332092—dc22
 [B]
                                                                    2011016783

eBook ISBN: 9781612281728

ABOUT THE AUTHOR: Karen Bush Gibson has written more than 30 educational books about famous people, different cultures, and historical events. She lives with her family in Oklahoma and has been a fan of University of Oklahoma football since they had another record-breaking running back, Billy Sims.

PUBLISHER'S NOTE: The following story has been thoroughly researched and to the best of our knowledge represents a true story. While every possible effort has been made to ensure accuracy, the publisher will not assume liability for damages caused by inaccuracies in the data, and makes no warranty on the accuracy of the information contained herein. This story has not been authorized or endorsed by Adrian Peterson.

TABLE OF CONTENTS

Words in **bold** type can be found in the glossary.

Adrian Peterson has been chosen to play in the Pro Bowl four times.
The Pro Bowl is professional football's All-Star game. Players are
chosen by other players, coaches, and football fans. In Peterson's first
Pro Bowl in 2008, he was chosen as the MVP (Most Valuable Player).

NFL's Best Running Back

By 2011, the Pro Bowl had a four-way tie for the most **rushing touchdowns**. When the game ended on January 30, the tie was over. Adrian Peterson of the Minnesota Vikings rushed for 14 yards to make his fourth Pro Bowl touchdown. With a total of 80 Pro Bowl rushing yards, he had broken another football record.

Breaking records seems to come naturally for this **running back**. When Peterson has the ball, all eyes are on his purple Number 28 jersey. He zooms past the other team. Often, he is untouchable.

In only his eighth NFL game, Peterson set a single-game NFL rushing record. The first Viking to win an NFL rushing title, he has been

In his fourth Pro Bowl, Peterson scored his fourth Pro Bowl touchdown. His league, the NFC (National Football Conference), won the Pro Bowl 55-41.

a leading rusher every season. It's no wonder he has been called the best running back in the National Football League (NFL).

With 5,782 rushing yards, Peterson made 52 touchdowns in the first four years of his professional (pruh-FEH-shuh-nul) career. He told *Sports News* in 2010, "I play this game to be the best player ever."

The Pro Bowl is an all-star football game in which the best football players play. Peterson had played in the Pro Bowl all four years of his professional football career. He has come a long way since the days of playing peewee football in his small hometown of Palestine, Texas.

Peterson calls track his second love after football. During the 2011 off-season, he practiced running 200-meter and 400-meter sprints. His dream is to compete in the Olympics.

"All Day"

Palestine is a small town with about 20,000 people. About 114 miles east of Dallas, Texas, it is known for piney woods—and for Adrian Peterson.

On March 21, 1985, a second boy was born to Bonita Brown and Nelson Peterson. They named him Adrian. When the boy was two years old, Nelson began calling him A.D. because he could run "All Day." The name soon caught on.

A.D. raced after his brother, Brian, who was 11 months older. Brian was riding his bike one day when he was nine. A drunk driver struck and killed him. A.D. saw it happen. Bonita told *Tulsa World* that Brian's death was hard on A.D. "When Brian passed, there was a big part of him that was gone because they did everything together."

Nelson Peterson decided that A.D. needed to do something with all his energy. He signed him up in peewee football, and Nelson became the team's assistant coach.

A.D. was a natural, which wasn't surprising since both of his parents were athletes. Nelson had played basketball, setting records as a guard for Idaho State University. Bonita had been a sprinting and jumping champion. She had earned a track **scholarship** (SKAH-lur-ship) to the University of Houston. She gave A.D. pointers, such as keeping his eye on the finish line. He couldn't beat his mother in a race until he reached the seventh grade. "It was kind of embarrassing. But, yeah, up until that time, Mom was smoking me. She could leave me in the dust," he told the Minneapolis-St. Paul *Star Tribune.*

Nelson was proud of his son, but he let A.D. know that good grades come first. A.D. found out how serious his dad was when he

Adrian Peterson takes after his parents, both college athletes. Nelson Peterson (left) remains the seventh highest scorer for the Idaho State University Bengals.

brought home his first F in the fifth grade. A.D. suited up for Saturday's game, but Nelson kept him on the sidelines, a first for the star peewee football player. With tears in his eyes, A.D. watched his team play.

Although Nelson did not live with A.D. and his mother, he was an active father. When A.D. was in junior high, everything changed. Nelson was arrested in 1998 for selling crack cocaine and **laundering** money. He was sentenced to ten years in prison.

Weekend phone calls with A.D. took the place of face-to-face parenting. "Just because you are [in jail] doesn't mean you can stop being a father," Nelson said.

A.D. stayed busy with sports: track and field in the spring and football in the fall. In track, he ran 100- and 200-meter events. His personal best came during his senior year of high school. He ran the 100-yard dash in just 10.33 seconds.

A.D. also competed in long jumps and triple jumps. "He [nearly] jumped clean out of the pit. I guarantee you he could be an Olympic long-jumper if he wasn't a football player," Coach Steve Eudey told *Tulsa World*.

A.D.'s talent at track and field was nothing compared to what he did as a **tailback** for the Palestine High School Wildcats. As a junior, he

A.D.'s mother and brother Jaylon Jackson joined A.D. on National Signing Day. Peterson had his choice of schools. Although many people in his Texas hometown hoped he would choose the University of Texas, Peterson went with the University of Oklahoma.

made 22 touchdowns and rushed for a total of 2,051 yards.

His senior year was even better. He scored 32 touchdowns and rushed for 2,960 yards. Voted National Player of the Year, Peterson became the number one college **recruit** (ree-KROOT) in the country.

Peterson became OU's first freshman running back to rush for 100 yards in a game. He averaged 148.1 yards per game in his first year at

Breaking NCAA Records

Darrell Wyatt, an assistant coach for the University of Oklahoma (OU) Sooners, was the East Texas recruiter. In 2002, he told OU about an amazing junior in Palestine—Adrian Peterson. With his father's advice, Peterson accepted their offer to play football for them. He arrived in Norman, Oklahoma, in June 2004.

According to former Sooner coach Chuck Long, young players like Peterson had to earn the respect of older players. He told *Sports Illustrated* in 2004, "Usually it takes some time. Like, a year." Peterson earned their respect within one month. He rushed for over 100 yards in each of his first three games. By the

fourth game, he had earned the right to start—
and ran for over 100 yards again.

By the end of his first season, Peterson
had rushed for 1,925 yards, an OU record for a
single season and a National Collegiate Athletic
Association (NCAA) record for a freshman.
He received All Conference and All-American
honors. He also came in second in Heisman
Trophy voting. No other freshman had ever
been runner-up for college football's top award.

On October 9, 2004, Peterson went with
Coach Bob Stoops to visit patients at Children's
Hospital. One of the patients was T.J. Hutchings,
a high school baseball pitcher who had Ewing's
sarcoma (sar-KOH-muh), a type of cancer.

T.J. wasn't happy about spending
his eighteenth birthday in the hospital for
treatments. He was told to come to the nursing
station. "I turned the corner, and Bob Stoops
and Adrian Peterson
were there. . . .
They brought out
the cake and

everything. It was pretty awesome," T.J. told *The Oklahoman.*

Peterson was looking forward to a home game against Iowa State. Scheduled for October 14, it would be the first football game his father had seen him play in eight years. Released from prison, Nelson was living and working in nearby Oklahoma City.

"Being able to [see my father] in the stands, maybe it'll give me the extra drive I need," Adrian told *Tulsa World.*

During the game, cameras showed Nelson cheering for his son. In the fourth quarter, Adrian ran for a touchdown. When he dived into the **end zone**, he broke his collarbone. He would sit out the rest of the regular season.

On January 1, 2007, Peterson played his last college football game, the Fiesta Bowl. When the game against Boise State went into overtime, Peterson scored his last college touchdown in a 43-42 loss. With 41 touchdowns in college football, Peterson became OU's third leading rusher of all time.

When growing up in Palestine, Peterson was a huge fan of Dallas Cowboys cornerback Deion Sanders (left). Sanders celebrated with Peterson after the Vikings made Peterson their first-round draft pick.

Lucky Number 7

On April 29, the first round of the 2007 NFL **draft** was under way. After six teams made their picks, it was the Minnesota Vikings' turn. They chose Oklahoma Sooner running back Adrian Peterson. He told *USA Today* about playing for the Vikings: "Hopefully I can make some history for some kids, young kids that follow." He also wondered how a Southerner like him was going to survive Minnesota winters. "When I got drafted here, that's the first crazy thought that went into my head," he told the *Star Tribune*. "I'd always heard how cold it is."

When the 2007 football season started, Peterson traded his #28 Sooners jersey for a #28 Vikings jersey. He gave the Vikings his

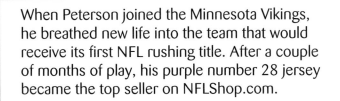

When Peterson joined the Minnesota Vikings, he breathed new life into the team that would receive its first NFL rushing title. After a couple of months of play, his purple number 28 jersey became the top seller on NFLShop.com.

best in the first game of the season. He was the leading rusher for that game and the next four. He averaged 121.4 yards per game.

The Chicago Bears were stunned when Peterson rushed for 224 yards against them, something no running back had ever been able to do. Three weeks later, Peterson set an NFL single-game rushing record against the San Diego Chargers with 296 yards. He finished the year with 1,341 rushing yards. He won the **Offensive Rookie** of the Year award and was picked for the Pro Bowl. He was also voted Pro Bowl MVP. It didn't take long for reporters to call Peterson the face of the Minnesota Vikings.

During his second season, his 1,760 rushing yards made him the leading rusher in the NFL. The Minnesota Vikings won the NFC North **Division** title that year.

In 2009, Peterson rushed for 1,383 yards. Although that was not as many as in 2008, he made 18 touchdowns, eight more than the year before. Division winners again, the Vikings lost the NFC Championship game to the New Orleans Saints in overtime.

Attending Adrian Peterson Day is so important to Peterson that he missed a **mandatory** mini weekend camp in 2009. He told the Minneapolis-St. Paul *Star Tribune*, "It was something that was already set up ahead of time before my mini camp schedule had come out.

Giving Back

Peterson lives in Eden Prairie, a **suburb** of Minneapolis. He shares his five-bedroom house with his brother Derrick, who keeps his schedule for him. Other family members and friends visit often. One of them is his daughter, Adeja. Born in 2004, she lives with her mother in Texas. Her lime green room has clouds painted on the ceiling.

Peterson stays busy both on and off the field. Besides spending time on **endorsement** deals, he works with several charities. He created the All Day **Foundation** to provide food and equipment for children in need. Adrian Peterson Day is held every year in Palestine.

Many events are held to collect food for families in need, and there's even a parade.

During the 2010 season, the Vikings' leading rusher looked for ways to do something about the 20 **fumbles** of his professional career. He watched tapes of himself. "That was the main thing I noticed when I looked at the fumbles I had: getting the ball away from my body," he told *Sports Illustrated*.

Peterson knew he had to hold the football higher and tighter, and it worked. He went from nine fumbles in 2008 to only one in 2010. He was fifth in rushing for the NFL. His 1,298 yards pushed his career rushing yards over 5,000. Peterson made the longest run of his career—80 yards—against the Detroit Lions on September 26.

In the 2010 season, the Vikings won six games but lost ten. It was the first time in three years they didn't make the playoffs.

The Vikings celebrated their 50th year in the NFL in 2010. During the December 19 celebration, Peterson was voted by fans as one of the 50 greatest Minnesota Vikings of all time.

In March 2011, Peterson took part in a 24-day trip to Africa with other NFL players on behalf of Starkey Hearing Foundation. They delivered 22,000 hearing devices to African children and adults. Two months earlier, Peterson had held an ice fishing benefit to raise money for the foundation.

Although he's known for zigzagging around players at top speed, he's not afraid to hit the opposing team head on. In a game against the Pittsburgh Steelers, Peterson ran over defensive back William Gay. "I just lowered my shoulder, kept my feet moving and um, you know . . . gave him the business."

His contract was nearing its end in 2011, and people wondered whether Peterson would stay with the Vikings or go with another team. He just wanted to prepare for the next football season. Like many NFL players, Peterson was not happy about the dispute between NFL owners and players before the 2011 football season. If he couldn't play football, he said he would not be able to "be the best player to ever play this game."

CAREER STATISTICS

Year	Team	G	ATT	RYDS	LNG	REC	RCYDS	RCLNG	TYDS	F	TD
2007	MIN	14	238	1,341	73	19	268	60	1,609	4	13
2008	MIN	16	363	1,760	67	21	125	16	1,885	9	10
2009	MIN	16	314	1,383	64	43	436	63	1,819	7	18
2010	MIN	15	283	1,298	80	36	341	34	1,639	1	13
Career		61	1,198	5,782	80	119	1,170	63	6,952	21	54

(G=Games played, ATT=Rushing attempts, RYDS=Rushing yards, LNG=Longest run, REC=Receptions, RCYDS=Receiving yards, RCLNG=Longest reception, TYDS=Rushing + receiving yards, F=Fumbles, TD=Touchdowns rushing + receiving)

CHRONOLOGY

1985 Adrian Peterson is born on March 21 in Palestine, Texas.

1992 His brother, Brian, is killed by a drunk driver.

1998 Adrian's father is sentenced to ten years in prison.

2003 Adrian wins the Hall Trophy as the best high school player in the nation.

2004 His daughter, Adeja, is born. He plays his first game as an OU Sooner on September 4. After the season, he is chosen as All-American and All-Conference. In the Heisman selection, Peterson is runner-up.

2007 On April 29, Peterson is drafted by the Minnesota Vikings. He plays his first NFL game on September 9. On October 14, he makes all-time third in most yards gained in a game with 361 yards against the Chicago Bears. He sets the NFL single-game rushing record with 296 yards and achieves 315 scrimmage yards for third all-time ranking on November 4.

2008 He is the leading rusher in the NFL with 1,760 yards.

2009 His rushing yards drop to 1,383, but he makes an impressive 18 touchdowns during the season.

2010 Peterson passes 5,000 in career rushing yards. The Vikings have to look for another place to play home games when the Metrodome caves in during a snowstorm on December 12. Peterson makes 12 touchdowns in the season and the longest single run of his career—80 yards. He is chosen as one of the 50 greatest Minnesota Vikings of all time.

2011 Playing in his fourth Pro Bowl in four years, Peterson sets a record with his fourth Pro Bowl touchdown.

FIND OUT MORE

Books

Currie, Stephen. *Adrian Peterson*. Broomall, PA: Mason Crest Publishing, 2008.

Doeden, Matt. *The World's Greatest Football Players*. Mankato, Minn.: Capstone Press, 2010.

Sandler, Michael. *Adrian Peterson*. New York: Bearport Publications, 2010.

Savage, Jeff. *Adrian Peterson*. Minneapolis: Lerner Publishing, 2010.

Stewart, Mark. *The Minnesota Vikings*. Chicago, IL : Norwood House, 2008.

Works Consulted

"Adrian Peterson vs. Adrian Peterson." *Sporting News*, December 17, 2007, Vol. 231 Issue 51, p. 59.

Aikman, Troy. "Peterson: He'll Break Your Hand and Break Your Team's Back." *Sporting News*, November 24, 2008, Vol. 232 Issue 45, p. 77.

Barkowitz, Ed. "Adrian Peterson's Fantasy Is to Join 2,000-yard Club." *Philadelphia Daily News*, September 10, 2009.

Brown, Clifton. "As Long As He's in the Playoffs, Peterson Figures He Might as Well Win." *Sporting News*, January 15, 2009, Vol. 233 Issue 1, p. 59

CBS Sports: Adrian Peterson http://www.cbssports.com/nfl/players/playerpage/517568/adrian-peterson

Craig, Mark. "Peterson Family Reflect on Back's Long, Hard Journey to NFL." Minneapolis-St. Paul *Star Tribune*, April 29, 2007.

Davis, Brian, and Gary Jacobson. "Adrian Peterson Looks Ahead to a Better Day for His Father." *Dallas Morning News*, October 4, 2006.

ESPN: Adrian Peterson. http://sports.espn.go.com/nfl/players/profile?playerId=10452

Evans, Thayer. "The Pride of Palestine: Texas Town Follows Its Star." *The New York Times*, September 23, 2007.

Gosselin, Rick. "Rookie Adrian Peterson Isn't All-Day Yet." *Dallas Morning News*, October 25, 2007.

Hack, Damon. "The Virtue of Patience." *Sports Illustrated*, October 15, 2007, Vol. 107 Issue 15, pp. 34–35.

Hoover, John. "Big Dreams: Adrian Peterson: Athletic Destiny." *Tulsa World*, August 20, 2006.

——. "Waiting for Dad: Adrian Peterson Will Play His First College Games in Front of His Father This Season." *Tulsa World*, June 30, 2006.

Jensen, Sean. "Everybody's Talking about Adrian Peterson." *Saint Paul Pioneer Press*, November 10, 2007.

Jock Bios: Adrian Peterson http://www.jockbio.com/Bios/Peterson/Peterson_facts.html

Kennedy, Kostya. "Ex-Oklahoma Running Back." *Sports Illustrated*, February 26, 2007, Vol. 106 Issue 9, pp. 30–31.

Murphy, Austin. "The Oklahoma Kid." *Sports Illustrated*, October 11, 2004, Vol. 101, Issue 14.

NFL: All-Time Records http://static.nfl.com/static/content/public/image/history/
    pdfs/Records/All_Time_Individual_Records.pdf
NFL History http://www.nfl.com/history
"The NFL's Top 100 Players." *Sporting News*, September 14, 2009, Vol. 233 Issue 21,
    p. 34.
Scoggins, Chip. "Adrian Peterson Leads the Vikings' Charge." Minneapolis-St. Paul
    Star Tribune, August 2, 2008.
——. "Adrian Peterson the First Viking to Win an NFL Rushing Title." Minneapolis-St.
    Paul *Star Tribune*, December 28, 2008.
Seifert, Kevin. "At Home on an October Day with Adrian Peterson." Minneapolis-St.
    Paul *Star Tribune*, November 6, 2007.
——. "A Wild Week for Adrian Peterson after Record-setting Game." Minneapolis-St.
    Paul *Star Tribune*, November 8, 2007.
Sooner Sports: Media Guides http://www.soonersports.com/sports/m-footbl/
    archive/media_guide.html
Souhan, Jim. "Adrian Peterson's Mother Still Maintains Strong Presence in Her Son's
    Life." Minneapolis-St. Paul *Star Tribune*, November 12, 2008.
Thompson, Trae. "Peterson Family Reunites on a Bittersweet Day for Adrian." *Fort
    Worth Star-Telegram*, October 14, 2006.
Vernon, Cheril. "Auction, Food Boxes Highlight Adrian Peterson Day Saturday."
    Palestine Herald, June 11, 2009.
Williams, Charean. " 'All Day' Impact: Adrian Peterson Quickly Takes the NFL by
    Storm with Speed, Power." *Fort Worth Star-Telegram*, October 11, 2007.
Zulgad, Judd. "Adrian Peterson Aims to Be Face of Vikings' Franchise." Minneapolis-St.
    Paul *Star Tribune*, May 15, 2008.

Videos

"Adrian Alllllll Day Peterson 2008 Highlights"
    http://www.youtube.com/watch?v=WVQiv4E0ExQ&feature=related
"Adrian Peterson Goes to the Minnesota Vikings"
    http://www.youtube.com/watch?v=pU6rx_q-iLQ&feature=related
"Adrian Peterson Moves . . ."
    http://www.youtube.com/watch?v=nD-wivXcHTQ
Adrian Peterson Videos
    http://www.adrianpeterson.com/videos

On the Internet

All Day Foundation
    http://www.alldayfoundation.org/
NFL: Adrian Peterson
    http://www.nfl.com/players/adrianpeterson/profile?id=PET260705
The Official Site of the Minnesota Vikings
    http://www.vikings.com/

GLOSSARY

division (dih-VIZH-un)—Any of the groups within the NFL that compete against each other in playoff games.

draft (DRAFT)—An annual event during which NFL teams choose college players to play for them; the teams with the worst records get the first choices.

endorsement (en-DORS-munt)—The public support of a product.

end zone (END ZOHN)—Either end of the football field where a team scores touchdowns.

foundation (fown-DAY-shun)—A group that raises money to help other groups or people.

fumble (FUM-bul)—The act of dropping the football during play.

laundering (LAWN-dur-ing)—A crime that makes money that was gained illegally look like it comes from legal sources.

mandatory (MAN-dih-tor-ee)—Required.

offensive (ah-FEN-siv)—From the part of the team that tries to score points.

recruit (ree-KROOT)—To get a person to join a group; also, a person who has been asked to join a group.

rookie (RUK-ee)—An athlete's first season on a college or professional team.

running back (RUN-ing BAK)—An offensive player who runs with the football.

rushing (RUH-shing)—Running with the football.

sarcoma (sar-KOH-mah)—A cancerous tumor.

scholarship (SKAH-lur-ship)—Money awarded to be used for school or college.

suburb (SUH-burb)—An area on the outer edges of a city.

tailback (TAYL-bak)—The offensive player farthest from the scrimmage line.

touchdown (TUTCH-down)—A goal in football that is worth six points.

INDEX